MW00395942

the
green crab
cookbook

To Paolo, Lorena, Angelo, Domenico, & Monica
of the Tagliapietra family

Edited by Mary Parks, Thanh Thái, and Contributors to the Green Crab R&D Project
Art direction, book design, and lettering by Mary Parks, Thanh Thái, and Julian Burlando-Salazar
Cover Illustration & Photography by © Anne Vetter (front and spine) and © Thanh Thái (back)

Interior illustrations by individual recipes authors (with exceptions noted below)

2018 Jamie Bassett, 6, 29, 112; 2018 Anne Vetter, 31; © 2018 Vitalii Hulai/ Adobe Stock, 14; © 2018 romantiche/ Adobe Stock, 16; © 2018 bbivirys/ Adobe Stock, 64; © 2018 Delicious/ Adobe Stock, 80; © 2018 michalrybski/ Adobe Stock, 121.

Library of Congress Cataloging-in-Publication Data available upon request.

IngramSpark
www.ingramspark.com
1-855-997-7275

Names: Parks, Mary, author. | Thái, Thanh, author.
Title: The Green Crab Cookbook: an Invasive Species Meets a Culinary Movement / Mary Parks and Thanh Thai.

ISBN 978-0-578-42794-2 (hardcover)
Subjects: CKB000000

Our deepest appreciation to Manomet and New Hampshire Sea Grant for their continued support and collaboration.

This book was produced entirely by volunteer effort, something we are incredibly grateful for. To our recipe writers, editors, and friends of the Green Crab R&D, we couldn't have done this without you. Thank you.

Masinette: green crab caviar

contents

a pre- molt crab

foreword

European green crabs invaded the east coast of North America in the early 1800s. Although they are not what we consider a 'new' invasive species in New England, they have had a devastating–and growing–impact on important coastal habitat and marine life. Green crabs are voracious predators of soft-shell clams and a driving force behind declining New England soft-shell populations. Their tendency to burrow into sediment has also lead to the destruction and disappearance of critical coastal habitat, such as salt marshes and eelgrass beds. To make matters worse, populations will likely increase as ocean temperatures rise.

This invader is not just a problem in New England. Green crabs have invaded the East and West coasts of the U.S. and Canada, South America, Australia, Africa, and Asia. It is one of the most 'successful' invasive species in the world. Although this crab has been in the eastern U.S. for over 200 years, we haven't found a solution for reducing their populations. However, many culinary entrepreneurs and environmentalists are now turning to the "if you can't beat 'em, eat 'em" strategy. Simply put, if green crabs are here to stay, why not benefit from them in some way? Creating a market demand for green crab products could also support the development of new fisheries and lead to a diversified source of income for New England fishermen. It's a win-win situation.

Many culinary products and markets hold great potential for green crabs. Soft-shell green crabs, known as *moeche* or *moleche*, are a delicacy in Venice, Italy. Venetian crab fishermen, or *moecante*, have been harvesting green crabs from the Venetian lagoon for centuries. Moecante target the Mediterranean green crab, a species that is very similar to the European green crab. In fact, to the naked eye these two species look identical.

The Venetian soft-shell green crab fishery depends entirely on the ability of fishermen to identify crabs that are about to shed their shell and become soft, a process known as molting. These crabs, called pre-molt crabs, are sorted from the rest of the catch and held in cages until they molt. Once they have molted, the soft crabs are sold live to local restaurants at anywhere from $25-$55 U.S. dollars per pound. This is an incredibly lucrative fishery. The soft-shell crabs are a popular deep-fried

Venetian molcche in a holding well

delicacy, served with chips or a wedge of polenta in many Venetian restaurants.

In 2017, I had the once-in-a-lifetime opportunity to travel to Venice to live and work with Paolo Tagliapietra and his family, who are multi-generational moecante. Paolo also hosted my partner, Chris Jamison, who is a Maine lobsterman. Chris and I were completely immersed in the Venetian green crab fishery during our stay, working from sunrise to sunset harvesting and sorting through hundreds of pounds of crabs. Every night we were treated to an amazing seafood feast prepared by the Tagliapietra family, including platters of delicious deep-fried soft-shell crab. We documented every detail of this trip so that we could attempt to adapt their fishery techniques (and recipes!) to create a similar fishery in New England.

Paolo demonstrates sorting crabs in the lagoon

The opportunity to work with the moecante was made possible by Jonathan Taggart, a fine arts conservator from Maine who happened to be working in Venice several years ago and asked the simple question "why aren't we doing this with our own invasive pest?" In three years, that single question would lead to extensive scientific and market research, numerous collaborations, recipe development, restaurant trials, meetings and workshops, and federal grant support awarded to Manomet and New Hampshire Sea Grant for developing a soft-shell fishery in New England. Perhaps the most impressive accomplishment to date was the successful production of soft-shell green crabs by both Jonathan and Chris in Maine in the summer of 2018, culminating with the first sale of soft-shell green crabs within the United States. The response from chefs and consumers was overwhelmingly positive and we look forward to the 2019 season.

Moeche for sale in Brunswick, ME

Of course, there are many other culinary uses of green crabs and therefore massive economic potential for untapped markets. At the end of the day, seafood markets and fisheries are driven by the individual consumer. Purchasing invasive, local or underutilized seafood drives up demand. Higher demand for a seafood product allows industries to scale and in turn increases accessibility to consumers. In 2018, most seafood markets and institutions do not carry green crabs. With your help as consumers, we hope to change that.

Now let's get cooking.

- **Marissa McMahan, Ph.D.**
  Senior Fisheries Scientist
  Manomet

Marissa leads a sorting demo in Georgetown, ME

glossary

Antennae: Sensory organs located by the crab's eyes and mouth.

Apron: The abdomen of the crab which is folded under the body. Apron shape is used to determine if a crab is male or female and is important when sorting crabs for caviar (see page 28 for male and female photos).

Carapace: The top portion of the shell which covers the body. In green crabs, each side of the carapace near the mouth and eyes has "five points", also known as marginal teeth.

Eye Stalks: Visual structures with eyes on the end.

Gills: The feathery respiratory organ located under the carapace.

Masinette: The Venetian word for green crab caviar or roe. Often a blend of meat and roe. Also known as "masanette".

Mazanette: The Italian word for green crab caviar or roe. Often a blend of meat and roe.

Moeche: The Venetian word for soft-shell green crab.

Moecante: Venetian green crab fishermen.

Moleche: The Italian word for soft-shell green crab.

Mouth Piece: The crab's "jaws", located between the eye stalks.

Mustard: A viscous, orange/yellow substance also known as the hepatopancreas.

FAQ

Are green crabs always green?

Nope! Despite their name, green crabs come in all colors of the rainbow and can be multi-hued.

What's the best way to ID a green crab?

If you see a crab with "five points" on each side of the face, it's likely a green crab.

How did they get here?

Green crabs were likely transported from Europe in the ballasts of ships.

How did they spread so quickly?

According to a 1995 study by Cohen and Carlton, a single female green crab can produce up to 185,000 eggs in a single year! After hatching, a larval green crab can drift in the water column for weeks and settle far from its parents.

Where am I most likely to find green crabs in the wild?

New England and Eastern Canada have some of the densest populations of green crabs; however, they've invaded almost every continent. They can be found in estuaries and intertidal regions. To avoid predation, green crabs often burrow into mud, sand or rocks.

How can I start crabbing for green crabs?

In many states, registering for a green crab permit is free. A boat is often not necessary when harvesting green crabs in small quantities. Learn how to start trapping green crabs at greencrab.org/act.

Where can I purchase green crabs?

You can often purchase green crabs in bulk from seafood distributors or directly from New England fishermen. Ask your local seafood market if they have access to green crabs–often their distributors will! Visit greencrab.org for sourcing information.

preparation & handling

PREPARATION METHODS

1. **Caviar/Masinette:** Seasonally available (often in the Fall), shucked from only female crabs
2. **Soft-Shell Crab/Moeche:** Seasonally available (often in the Spring/ Summer)
3. **Stock & Broth:** Can be prepared year-round
4. **Meat/Hard-Shell Recipes:** Can be prepared year-round

PROCESSING

- Some of these recipes call for picking apart and preparing live crabs. To make the process easier, try freezing the crabs for at least 2 hours or until the crabs are completely still.
- We recommend wearing gloves when sorting green crabs. You'll avoid getting pinched and have an easier time picking up crabs.
- No gloves? Hold the crab with two fingers firmly on the outer points of the carapace to prevent a pinch.
- Always thoroughly rinse hard-shell crabs prior to cooking.

STORAGE

- Green crabs can survive for weeks out of water so proper storage and containment is very important. To prevent escape & possible reintroduction, ensure they are stored in a sturdy container with air-holes. A crab basket, burlap sack or plastic storage container with holes will work well.
- Keep crabs in the fridge or comparably cool space and use within 1 week.
- If purchasing directly from a fisherman, ensure your green crabs aren't stored with other species or fish racks.

monitoring green crabs with **citizen science**

It is important to know when and where the highest concentrations of green crabs can be found when developing a green crab fishery. Therefore, potential fishers can more efficiently fish for these crustaceans and researchers can more accurately track their removal efforts. Additionally, to develop a soft-shell fishery in the U.S. we need to deepen our understanding of the crab's molting patterns. In Venice, the soft-shell market has a distinct season that begins when a large concentration of green crabs become "pre-molt," or ready to molt. Understanding when and where large concentrations of "pre-molts" occur in the U.S., is necessary for the development of a soft-shell green crab industry. Monitoring green crab populations and pre-molts throughout estuarine and coastal New Hampshire allows the NH Green Crab Project to map where these crabs are found throughout the year while also increasing green crab awareness, education, and citizen science engagement.

The monitoring element of the NH Green Crab Project is known as the "Great Green Crab Hunt" and it is administered in partnership with NH Sea Grant's Coastal Research Volunteers and UNH Cooperative Extension's Nature Groupie (see photos on next page).

The hunts are open to the public and are held once a month between April and October. Citizen scientists are trained how to use a data collecting app and collect measurements, how to handle and identify crabs, and how to distinguish between males and females. The Great Green Crab Hunt involves citizen scientists collecting data in the field using a mobile app from ArcGIS Online called Survey 123. This allows us to collect data in real-time and generate a web map with photographic data. This map is public and a great tool to use with younger citizen scientists who can see their data being used in real time. Crowd-sourcing the green crab population mapping strategy serves several purposes including education, awareness, and engagement of the scientific and general community. It also serves as a data management and housing tool that can be accessed by the public to gain better understanding of the size, distribution, and seasonality of the green crab population.

With your help, we can deepen our understanding of green crabs and help jumpstart a commercial fishery. Visit page 127 to learn more about becoming involved.

- **Gabriela Bradt, Ph.D.**
  Fisheries Extension Specialist
  New Hampshire Sea Grant
  UNH Cooperative Extension

What can we learn from **cua đồng?**

WRITTEN & PHOTOGRAPHED BY THANH THÁI

Cua đồng, known as "rice paddy crabs" or "rice-field crabs", can be found across Vietnam and Southeast Asia and include several species of closely related crab. Even though several cua đồng species are native to the region, they are largely regarded as pests. Cua đồng thrive in rice paddy habitat and over the centuries their populations rapidly expanded with rice paddy development. As cua đồng became more prevalent, rice farmers noticed the crabs were damaging rice shoots while foraging, posing a major threat to their crop yields. Despite being a freshwater species, this behavior is similar to that of the green crab slicing through eelgrass.

The parallels between cua đồng and green crabs extend far beyond their foraging behavior. Both are similar in size and flavor profile and therefor can be processed with similar techniques. However, we can also look to the destructive impact of cua đồng and how that impact has been lessened by the development of a culinary market.

After populations of cua đồng grew, Vietnamese people began incorporating the crabs in their cuisine. Soon rice paddy crab dishes became popular across the country and populations of the once destructive crabs stabilized. Today, bún riêu (Vietnamese crab noodle soup, see page 67) is one of the country's most iconic dishes.

In creating a market for cua đồng, Vietnamese converted an agricultural dilemma into an accessible food source. Constant removal through culinary demand has mitigated the crabs' destruction of

Vietnamese rice paddies. In turn, the cua đồng fishery serves as an exemplary model for the invasive green crab movement.

From bún riêu (Vietnamese crab noodle soup) to cua rang muối (salt and pepper crab), this cookbook incorporates a variety of techniques and recipes that originally use cua đồng but substitute green crab because of their similarities. We hope this cookbook is a starting point for substituting other species with green crabs and learning to cook with small crabs.

Cua Rang Muối
Recipe on page 101

Bún Riêu
Recipe on page 67

basics

PREPARING MASINETTE

GREEN CRAB CAVIAR

BY ROGER WARNER & JONATHAN TAGGART

Italian: mazanetta/ mazanette (plural)
Venetian: masinetta/ masinette (plural)
(alt. spelling) masanetta/ masanette (plural)

In Venice, female green crabs are often shucked for masinette: a tangy & savory blend of green crab roe and meat. To note, regional Venetian and Italian spellings may vary but throughout this cookbook we will be using "masinette", a common Venetian spelling. This caviar is often sautéed with olive oil and white wine or served on an open shell with a squeeze of lemon. The following recipe details the basic method for shucking and preparing masinette. However, many of our recipes incorporate the delicacy: from Golden Caviar Pâté (see page 80) to New England Style She-Crab Soup (see page 64).

Linguine & masinette
Recipe on page 118

Harvesting Tip: Our taste testers believe the best time to harvest masinette in New England is between mid October and late November. This time frame may vary slightly with location and from year to year.

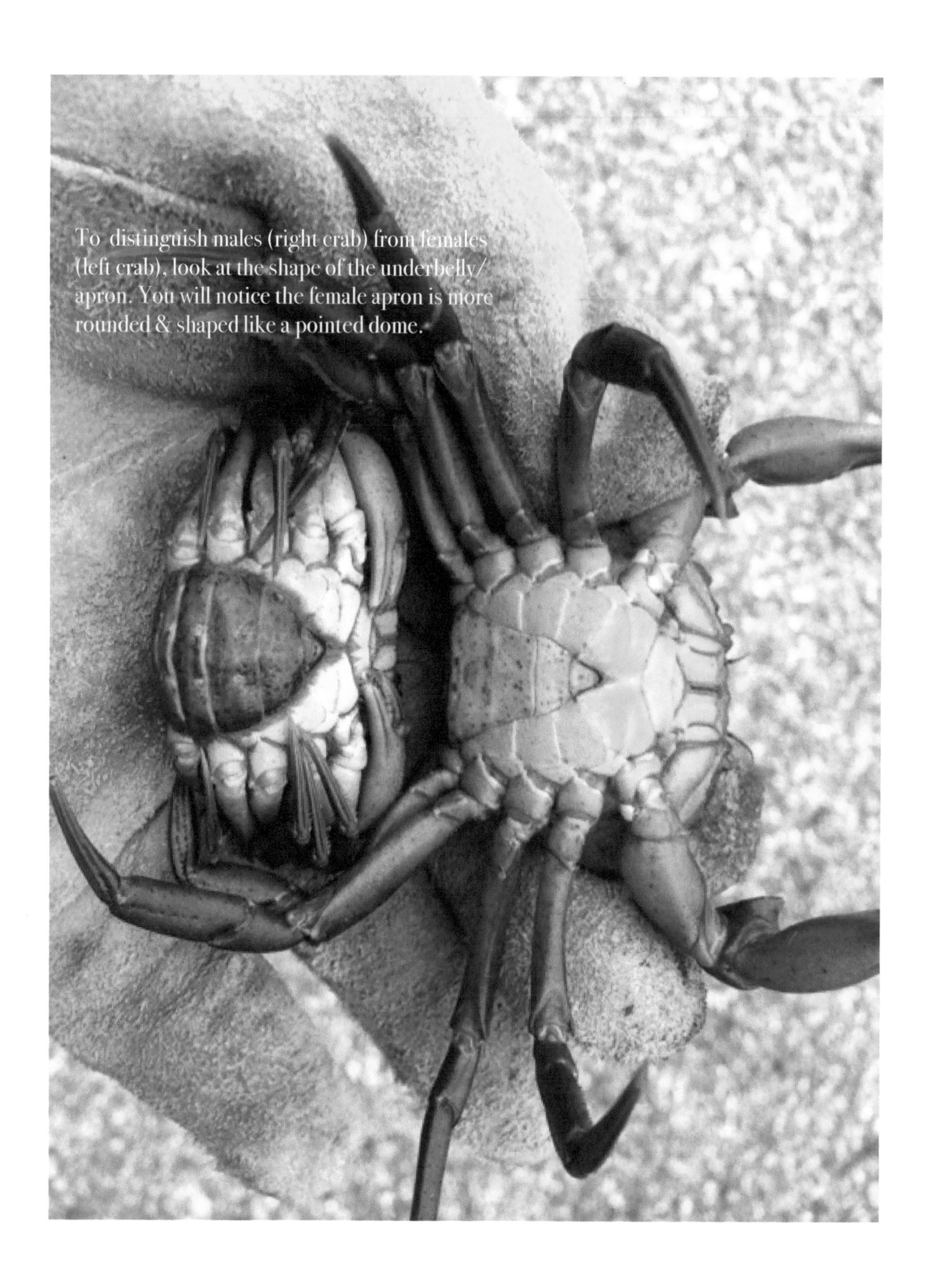

To distinguish males (right crab) from females (left crab), look at the shape of the underbelly/apron. You will notice the female apron is more rounded & shaped like a pointed dome.

MATERIALS & INGREDIENTS

- rubber gloves (for sorting live crab)
- large pot
- large skillet
- tapered chopstick, preferably metal
- tongs
- spatula
- colander
- 20-40 female green crabs
- extra virgin olive oil to taste
- splash of white wine/ lemon juice/ vinegar of choice
- pinch of salt & pepper

INSTRUCTIONS

1. With rubber gloves, vigorously rinse the crabs. Then separate the crabs by sex, using the shape of the triangle on the undersides.

   Note: Leftover male crabs and scraps can be used for stocks (see pages 50 & 53).

2. Boil female crabs for 6 minutes, remove and dry on a rack or baking sheet.

3. With your thumbnail, lift the back of the upper shell (carapace) and hinge it forward (picture instructions begin).

4. Scoop the meat and any orange caviar from the inside, forward edge of the upper shell using a chopstick, flat knife, or crab knife. Press hard against the shell when scooping to get the most meat.

5. Remove the triangle or "apron" from the underside of the crab.

6. Push the thin end of the chopstick into the aperture, covered by the triangle, to reveal the orange caviar.

7. Serve in one of two ways:

   Open-Shell: Serve masinette in the upper shell with lemon and olive oil (see photo in recipe intro).

   Classic Masinette: Sauté diced shallots in olive oil on high then add masinette. Reduce with a splash of white wine, lemon juice or vinegar and cook for 4 minutes.

3

4

5

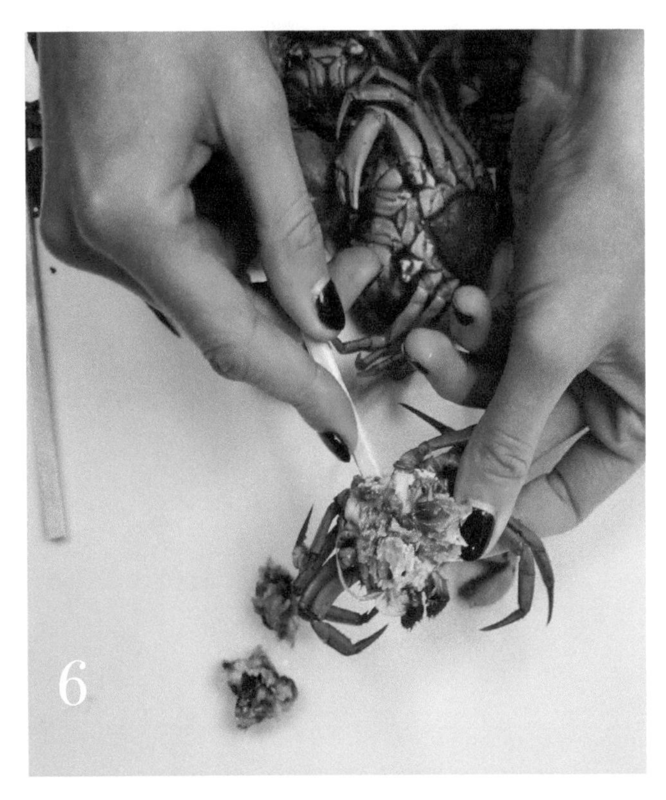
6

MOECHE

VENETIAN SOFT-SHELL GREEN CRAB

BY JONATHAN TAGGART

Italian - molecca/moleche (plural)

Venetian - mocca/moeche (plural)

It was love at first bite; crispy and crunchy, juicy and salty, tasting like the sea. Prepared deep fried, moeche, soft shell green crabs, have been a product of the Venetian lagoon for centuries. They are a delicious delicacy produced in limited quantities by the hard work of specialized fishermen known as molecante or moecante.

I have been fortunate enough to work a number of times in Venice on historic preservation and documentation projects. I ate my first moeca in 1997 when I was working with Professor Fabio Carerra. Since then, I always hoped it was moeche season when I had an opportunity to return to Venice. In 2015, I learned of efforts to restore non-productive clam flats with netting to prevent predation by ever-growing populations of invasive green crab. Georgetown, Maine, like many coastal New England towns, has witnessed steady declines in soft-shell clam populations, which many scientists believe is attributed to the green crab invasion. I didn't think much more about the crab until I was back in Venice that fall, eating moeche. I then began to wonder "Why aren't we producing moeche in Maine?"

Moleche on sale at an Italian fish market

Back in Maine, I sought scientists involved in green crab research to see what work could and has been done to produce soft-shell green crabs. My friend and marine scientist, Marissa McMahan, soon secured funding for green crab molting research to begin looking into how Venetian techniques could be applied to our invasive green crabs. I also became acquainted with Professor Sophie St. Hilaire, Ph.D., the first person to produce moeche in North America on Prince Edward Island. Her doctoral student, Luke Poirer, said "if you want to learn to make moeche, you must find a Venetian fisherman willing to teach."

Moecante have a reputation of being very secretive about their work. Back in Venice, I connected with Kees van den Meiracker and with fisher Rita Fortin. They agreed to reach out to any English speaking moecante they knew who might be willing to mentor me. That is how I met Paolo, Angelo, and Domenico in the spring of 2016. Paolo laughed when I mentioned how secretive moecante were supposed to be. He said "I'll tell you all our secrets! If you want to produce moeche, you will have to work as hard as we do. And if you work as hard as we do, you are our friend." Paolo became my mentor, taking me out into his office, the Venetian lagoon, with the Dolomite mountains in the background and began my lessons.

Producing moeche is an art and a science. It is more than fishing, and not quite aquaculture. Crabs have to molt and discard their old shells to grow. For a short period of time after molting, their new, larger shell is soft. At that moment they are a delicacy, cooked and eaten whole.

The concept is simple: capture crabs, wait until they molt, then eat them. The reality is complicated. It is an art that takes patience, knowledge, hard work, and the right place and time of the year. After the crabs have been captured, the key is sorting. The key to sorting is recognizing the molting signs. The molting signs are subtle, and change as the crab gets closer to molting. All crabs molt but it is easiest to recognize the signs in the males because they molt around springtime every year. Crabs within a day or two of molting look and act different. They need to be separated from the general population to reduce the chance of being cannibalized by their hungry, harder brethren. Once molted, they remain soft for a day or two before hardening. If they are not too soft, they can live out of water, refrigerated, for more than two weeks without hardening.

A Venetian stray inspects a pre-molt crab

Marissa and I produced our first batch of soft-shell green crabs later that spring. Excited about our success, we managed to convince Paolo to come to Maine that summer to work with us. However, he warned we may not be able to produce moeche into the warmer months, being the wrong time of year for molting males. To his surprise, when he looked at the crabs we were holding he exclaimed "this female will molt tomorrow!" and it did. On returning to Venice, he began experimenting with molting females and has now revised the old lost art of molting females. In the spring of 2017, Marissa and Georgetown fisherman, Chris Jamison, went to work with Paolo and family, to learn from the masters. In the summer of 2018 Chris became the first person in the US to produce and sell soft shell green crabs to restaurants.

There is so much work to be done but these efforts are an important first step. We hope that by substantially increasing the production of moeche on US shores, we can kickstart an artisanal industry and begin to mitigate the crab's spread and invasive impact.

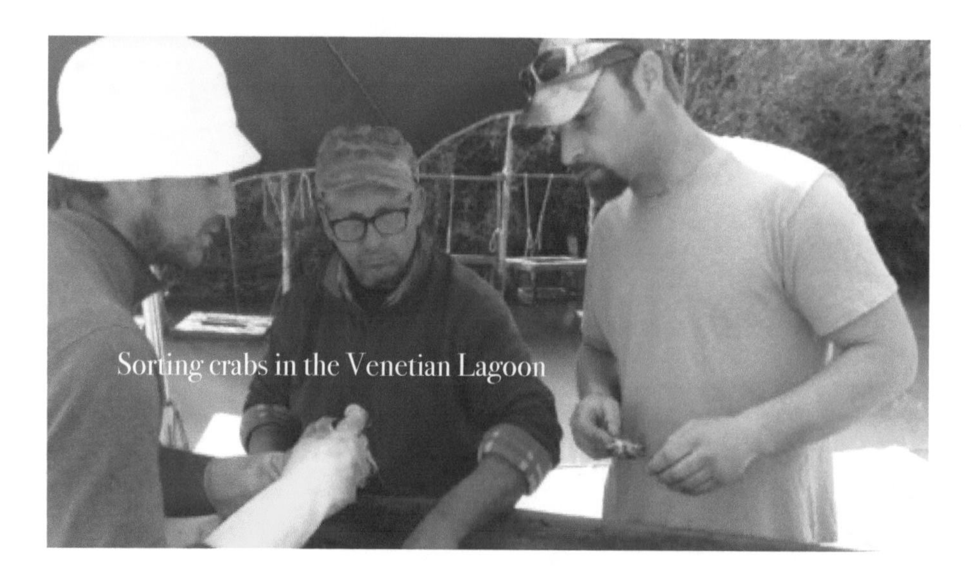

Sorting crabs in the Venetian Lagoon

Venetian moeche with polenta & lemon

INGREDIENTS

- 4-6 soft-shell green crab (moeche in Venetian)
- oil for frying (peanut, sunflower, vegetable etc.)
- salt & fresh cracked pepper to taste
- milk, saltwater, or seawater
- white flour

INSTRUCTIONS

1. Begin by filling a Dutch oven or large pot with 3 inches of oil, then heat to 360°.

2. If necessary, thoroughly rinse the soft-shell crabs in cold water. In Venice, moeche are usually fried directly after being removed from the lagoon.

3. Dip the crabs in milk, saltwater, or seawater (all Venetian methods), then dredge them in flour and seasoning.

4. Fry in batches of 4 to 6 crabs for 2 to 3 minutes or until golden brown. Flip the crabs with a pair of chopsticks and fry for an additional 2 minutes.

5. Remove from oil onto wire rack or towel.

   Optional: Serve with polenta, fresh lemon, & parsley.

SOUTHERN STYLE

SOFT-SHELL GREEN CRAB

BY THANH THÁI

In Venice, soft-shell green crab, or moeche, are fried whole and often dredged in milk or lagoon water depending on the recipe. This method of preparation may seem incomplete to those who are used to cooking with larger blue crabs, which are often trimmed and prepped before being deep fried and seasoned in a variety of ways. While the step is not necessary, trimming the crab prior to frying eliminates some of the shell's texture and produces a meatier bite. Coating the crabs in spiced harina flour also gives the shell a nice crisp.

INGREDIENTS

- oil for frying (peanut, sunflower, vegetable etc.)
- ½ cup masa harina (corn flour)
- ⅛ tsp turmeric powder
- ¼ tsp salt
- ½ tsp freshly ground white pepper
- 15-20 soft-shell green crabs

INSTRUCTIONS

Prepare Green Crabs

1. Wash the live crabs in cold water and drain.

2. Trim off the face & pointy ends of the legs (picture instructions begin).

   Note: See tips for preparing live crabs on page 16.

3. Open up the apron and trim at the base.

4. Lift each side of the carapace and trim off the gills.

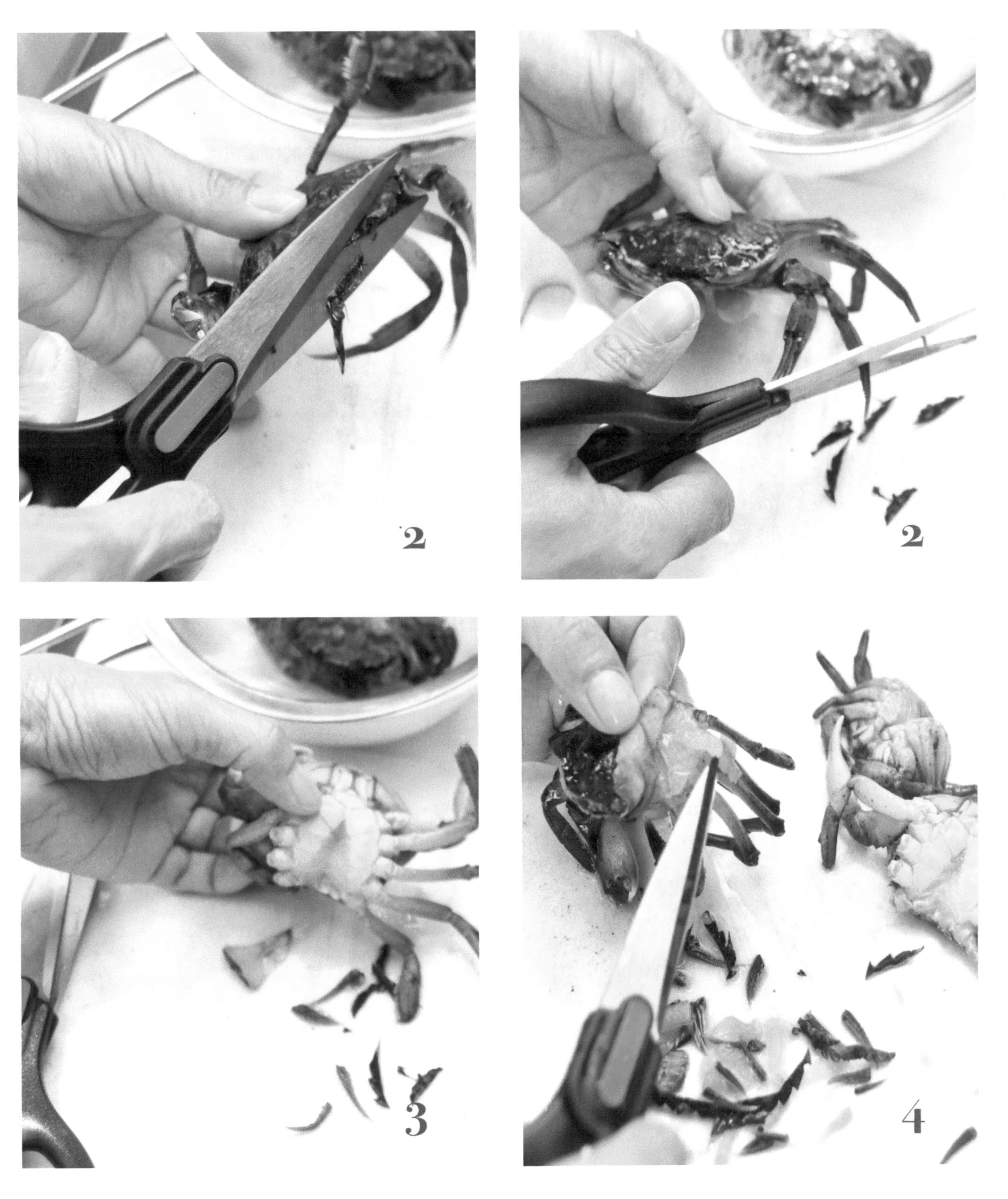
2
2
3
4

Fry Crabs

1. Preheat the oil in a pot or fryer until the temperature reaches 350° - 375°.

   Note: You can test your oil for readiness by frying a piece of trimmed crab. If the oil is hot and ready, the piece will sizzle and cook quickly.

2. Mix the dry ingredients including masa harina, turmeric powder, salt, and pepper. Then sift all the ingredients using a fine strainer.

3. Gently tap the side of the strainer with your palm. Discard any large pieces left in the strainer.

4. Once the oil is hot, coat 1-2 crabs at a time on both sides with seasoned flour, shake off excess flour and gently drop them in the pot or fryer.

   Note: For a crispier fry, dip the crabs in a whisked egg prior to coating with seasoned flour.

5. Turn the crabs a few times to prevent them from burning and let them fry for about 2-3 minutes or until golden brown.

6. Remove the crabs and place them in a strainer or on clean paper towels.

7. Serve hot and season according to taste. For a Chesapeake inspired dish, pair with lemon wedges and Old Bay!

PICKING GREEN
CRAB MEAT

BY THANH THÁI

With a sweet flavor and delicate texture, green crab meat can be used as a base or add-in for a variety of recipes. Try using green crab meat in your favorite lump crab, rock crab, or dungeness crab meat recipes. When removing green crab meat, I recommend using larger green crabs that measure at least 2 inches across the carapace. Removing the meat can be difficult with smaller crabs. The freshly picked crab meat, roe, and crab mustard may be kept sealed in a glass or ceramic container in the refrigerator up to 2-3 days or sealed tightly in plastic wrap and a freezer bag for up to 3 months.

INGREDIENTS & MATERIALS

- large green crabs
- nut/lobster cracker
- small knife (max ½ inch width)
- large green crabs (male or female)
- large pot for steaming crabs

INSTRUCTIONS

1. Thoroughly scrub and clean live crabs in cold water.
2. Steam the crabs for 7 minutes or boil for 6 minutes.
3. Once cooled, remove the carapace (upper shell) and scoop out the roe (picture instructions begin on next page).
4. Discard the carapace and crab mustard if desired.
5. Gently pull off the apron to remove the intestine and discard.
6. Use a knife to cut the body into 4 sections.

7. Remove the meat between the cartilage and save. Discard the gills, cartilage, shell bits, and any non-edible parts.

8. Use a nut/lobster cracker to crack or break the shell of the claw and remove the meat. Discard any shell bits.

9. Remove and discard the cartilage located inside the middle of the claw. Remove the claw meat.

10. When finished, look through the meat, remove and discard any shell or cartilage.

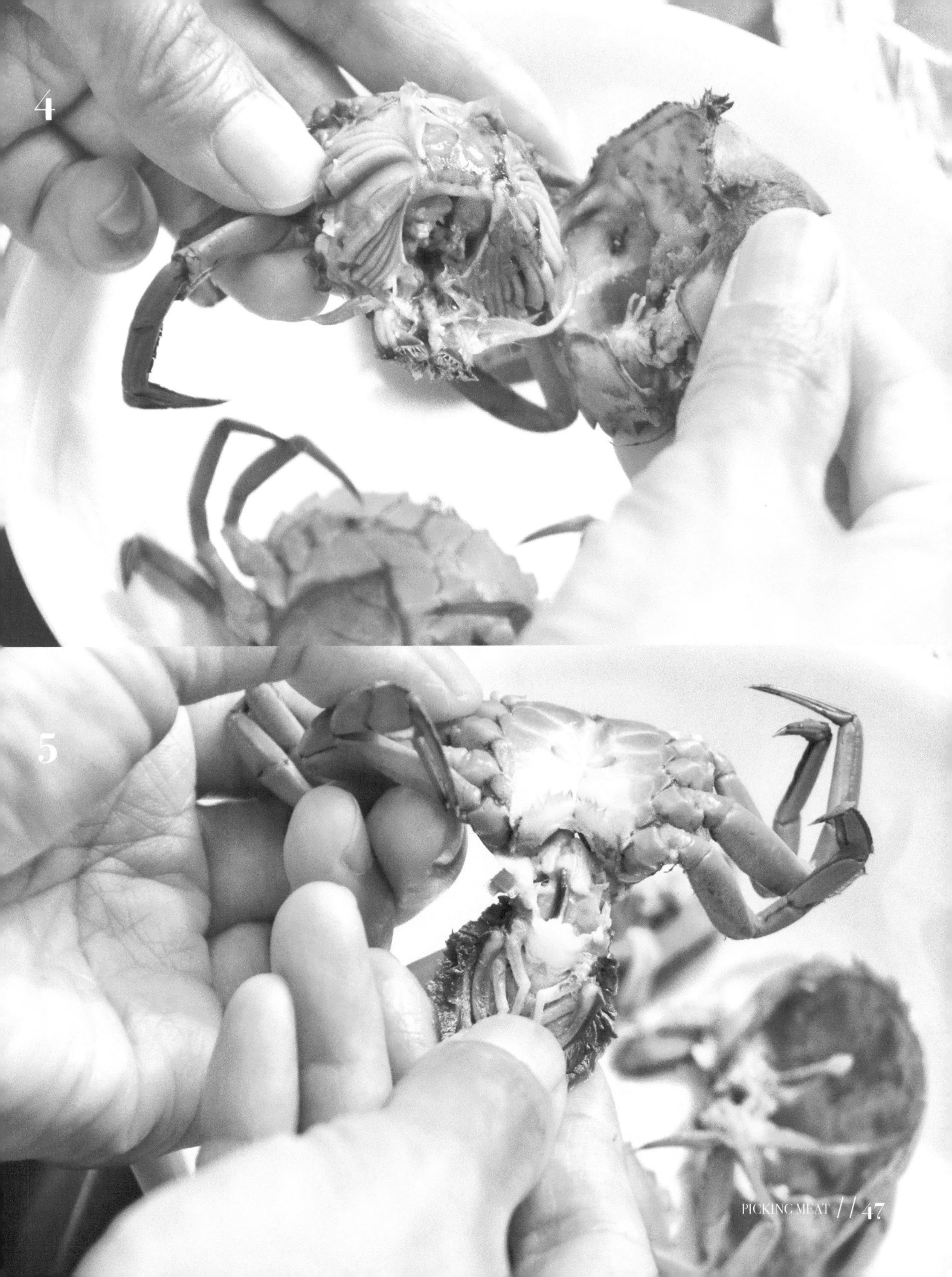
4
5

6
7

8
9

SIMPLE STOCK

BY ROGER WARNER

Stock is one of the simplest and most versatile green crab recipes. It can be made any time of year, from either male or female green crabs. You may also use crabs leftover from picking masinette or meat (see pages 26 & 43). This stock is fantastic for creating flavorful broths, but can also add depth to pasta dishes, vegetables, paellas, grains, and risottos. Naturally occurring umami compounds give green crab stock a unique, savory flavor profile, making it an excellent addition to seafood and non-seafood dishes.

INGREDIENTS & MATERIALS

- large pot for steaming crabs
- 1 lb of green crabs (minimum)
- sea salt to taste
- 3 Tbsp lemon juice
- mallet/rolling pin
- optional: lemon rind, 4 sprigs of thyme, 2 bay leaves & 5 cloves of crushed garlic

The flavor of the broth may vary with the season and crab size. For example, we've found smaller crabs harvested in Ipswich (shown in photo) produce a tangier broth than larger crabs harvested on Cape Cod.

Photo by Julian Burlando-Salazar

INSTRUCTIONS

1. Thoroughly rinse the live crabs in cold water twice.

2. Fill the pot so that the crabs are covered in 1 inch of water. Then add a hefty pinch of salt.

3. Add the crabs and bay leaves to boiling water, then boil just until the crabs turn red.

4. Use a mallet, rolling pin, or a similar object to crush the crabs within the pot. The finer the crabs are crushed, the more intense their flavor will be.

   Optional: add lemon juice, thyme and crushed garlic.

5. Turn the burner back on and allow the crushed crabs to simmer for at least 15 minutes.

6. Pour the stock over a fine strainer and into a container to cool.

7. Store in an airtight container for up to 5 days or freeze for later use.

For an added punch, try this recipe with female crabs during the caviar season or leftover crabs from shucking masinette.

GINGER & KELP STOCK

BY THANH THÁI

Unlike our classic stock recipe, this version involves some additional preparation. Without mustard and roe, the flavor of this stock is more subtle than our previous recipe. Adding kelp also gives the stock body. The process of cleaning the hard-shell crabs for making stock is similar to preparing Southern Style Soft-Shell Crabs (see page 39). The major difference is leaving the pointy legs intact but removing the entire carapace to separate the roe and mustard, which can be saved to use in another dish later.

INGREDIENTS

- 15 green crabs
- 2 ½ cups water
- 3 slices of ginger, ¼ inch thick, washed, lightly smashed
- 1 piece of fresh or dried kelp (8-10 inches)

INSTRUCTIONS

Prepare Green Crabs

1. Wash the live crabs in cold water and drain.

2. Remove and discard the carapace, gills, and apron. For female crabs, remove the roe and reserve it to cook another dish (see photos to right).

   Note: See tips for preparing live crabs on page 16.

3. Clean the crabs again by sprinkling about 2 tsp of salt on the prepared crabs and gently rubbing them. Wash the crabs in cold water 2-3 times to remove the salt and let them drain in a strainer.

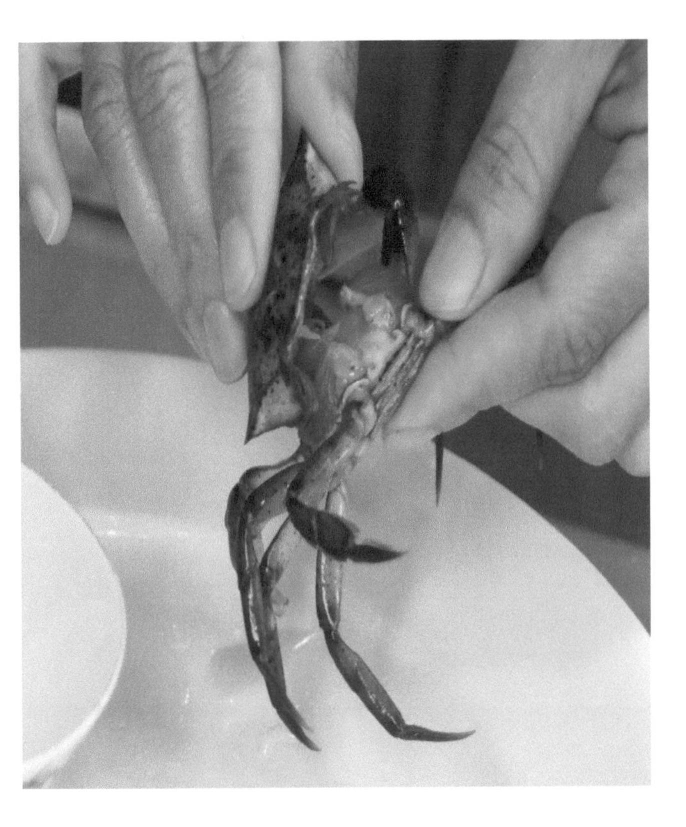

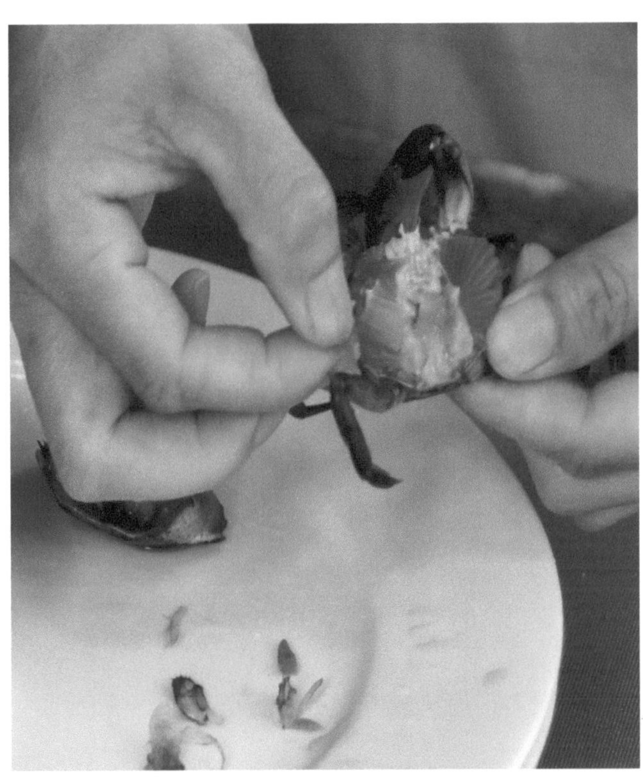

Prepare Stock

4. Crush the prepared crabs in a pot then add water, ginger, and kelp (photo instructions begin).

   Note: The finer the crabs are crushed, the more intense the flavor will be.

5. Turn the heat to high. Once boiling, decrease the heat to a simmer for about 20-25 minutes.

   Note: Watch your pot and turn the heat down if needed to prevent the liquid from boiling over.

6. Skim and discard the impurities (foam) that float to the top. Then strain the stock into a bowl using a fine strainer.

7. Add salt and seasoning of your choice.

8. Use this stock right away, or pour cooled contents into a sealed container and keep refrigerated for up to 2-3 days or frozen for up to 1-2 months.

   Note: We recommend keeping the stock unseasoned if freezing.

Processing Tip: Have leftover male crabs from preparing masanette? Remaining crabs can be used in stock recipes!

4

5

6

soups & stews

CIOPPINO

BY THANH THÁI

Cioppino is an Italian-American dish typically made with a fisherman's daily catch. I've made this type of stew a number of times over the years. Its contents mainly depend on what is available in my kitchen, what is fresh at my local market's seafood counter, and what my local fishermen are pulling up. In this recipe, I used local lobsters, squid, scallops, and green crab meat and stock.

INGREDIENTS

- 5 plum tomatoes
- 3 Tbsp chopped flat leaf parsley
- 1 cup ginger & kelp stock (see page 53)
- 1 large shallot or 1 small onion, minced
- 2-3 Tbsp vegetable oil
- 5 garlic cloves, smashed & minced
- 1-2 tsp dried chili flakes
- 6 fresh thyme sprigs
- 2 sausages (your choice)
- 10 oz firm fish (filleted & cut into 2 inch pieces)
- 1 lobster (~1 ½ - 2 lbs)
- 8 shrimp, peeled & deveined
- 8 sea scallops
- 8 oz cleaned squid (cut into bite-sized pieces)
- 4 oz green crab meat (see page 43)
- ½ cup red wine
- 2 Tbsp fish sauce (nước mắm in Vietnamese)
- 1 tsp sugar

Green Crabs & Lobsters: Lobster and green crab compete for the same food sources. As green crab populations increase in the Gulf of Maine, researchers worry the invasive could do major harm to the lucrative lobster industry.

INSTRUCTIONS

1. Peel the tomatoes by making a little cross with a sharp knife on the non-stem sides and dropping them in boiling water for about 20 seconds.

2. Remove the tomatoes from water when you see a small split on the side, then peel off the skins and discard. Cut the tomatoes in half and discard the core and seeds.

3. Dice all of the tomatoes.

4. In a blender, puree half of the tomatoes with the parsley and a little broth then set aside.

5. Gently boil the lobster in a little water for about 10 minutes, covered. Watch the stove to prevent the water from boiling over. Turn off the heat after the lobster is cooked and then discard the lobster water.

6. Once the lobster is cool enough to handle, remove the head (or lobster body) from the tail.

7. Remove and discard the intestines from the tail section. Then cut the tail meat into bite-size pieces and split the body in half and reserve to garnish later, if you wish.

8. In a large pan or pot, sauté garlic, onion/shallot, chilies, and thyme in oil until the onion/shallot are soft.

9. Add sausages and fish then sauté for about 2 minutes.

10. Add shrimp, scallops, and squid, then sauté for about 1 minute. Remove from heat and set aside.

11. Pour the puréed contents, wine, broth, and the remaining diced tomatoes into the pan or pot.

12. Let the contents simmer for about 15 minutes until the wine has cooked off and the broth is slightly reduced.

13. Add the fried sausages and fish to the pot. Cook until the seafood and sausages are cooked through.

14. Add the rest of the seafood and cook for 5 minutes.

15. Season with fish sauce and sugar.

16. Serve hot with fresh ground pepper and crusty bread.

NEW ENGLAND STYLE

SHE-CRAB SOUP

BY ROGER WARNER & JONATHAN TAGGART

She-Crab Soup is a staple of Charleston, South Carolina and a coastal favorite from the Chesapeake Bay to Louisiana. While it is traditionally made with the roe and meat of blue crabs, we have used green crab meat and roe to give the classic dish a New England take. The sweet and tangy flavor of the masinette gives the dish an unexpected punch. Cozy up with a cup of New England She-Crab Soup to celebrate the fall caviar season.

INGREDIENTS

- 4-6 Tbsp butter
- 3 Tbsp all-purpose flour
- 1 small onion, grated
- 3 cloves garlic, minced
- salt & pepper to taste
- 2 or 3 quarts whole milk
- 1 ½ cups simple stock (see page 50)
- ½ cup sherry wine (or to taste)
- Old Bay seasoning to taste
- Worcestershire sauce to taste
- hot sauce to taste
- 2 sprigs fresh dill
- ½ cup masinette (see page 26)
- ½ cup green crab meat (see page 43)
- chives for garnish

INSTRUCTIONS

1. In a large stockpot, melt all the butter and sauté the garlic and onion until translucent. Stir in the flour to make a smooth paste or roux. Cook for about 3 minutes, whisking constantly.

2. Gradually whisk in the milk so that no lumps form and then stir in the green crab stock.

3. Bring to a simmer, and pour in ¾ of the sherry. Season with dill, Worcestershire sauce, and hot sauce.

4. Cover and simmer for about 30 minutes, until soup has reduced by ⅓.

5. Add desired amount of masinette and green crab meat then simmer for a few minutes.

6. Ladle the soup into bowls, and top off with a splash of the remaining sherry and a sprinkle with fresh chives or greens of choice. Season with salt, pepper, and Old Bay to your taste.

The soup can be stored for up to two days and frozen for up to two months.

BÚN RIÊU

VIETNAMESE CRAB NOODLE SOUP

BY THANH THÁI

"Bún riêu" is a crab noodle soup that is incredibly popular across Vietnam. The soup is typically made with a crab known as cua đồng but can also be made with invasive green crabs, which are similar in size and flavor profile to the rice paddy crab.

The stock or broth used in this soup is made using the traditional Vietnamese method of crushing crabs by hand. Unlike our previous stock recipes (see pages 50 & 53), this method involves crushing the crabs to a pulp to extract as much meat as possible. I recommend adding a handful of crabs to a freezer bag and crushing them with a heavy object; however, you can also use food processor to expedite the process.

Bún riêu is typically eaten with a large platter of fresh herbs, vegetables and a side of fish sauce and fine shrimp sauce. In this recipe, I used banana blossom, water spinach, bean sprouts, culantro, mint, perilla, Thai basil, Vietnamese mint or lemon balm, lime, and hot chili peppers. If you do not have access to banana blossom or the water spinach, substitute them with finely shredded green or red cabbage. When I sit down to eat my bowl of noodles and broth, I add a lot of the vegetables from my plate, extra chilies, a little shrimp sauce, a drizzle of fish sauce, and a squeeze of lime or lemon juice. Then I mix it all up and slurp it down while it is piping hot!

MATERIALS & INGREDIENTS

Materials

- 1 large pot (minimum 20 cups)
- 2 large freezer bags
- skimmer spoon
- rock, mallet or food processor

Noodle Soup

- 40-50 green crabs (minimum), crushed
- 12 cups cold water
- 3 Tbsp annatto oil :

  3 ½ Tbsp canola oil & 1 Tbsp annatto seeds
- 2-3 large shallots, chopped (about ¾ cup)
- 2 large garlic cloves, smashed & chopped
- ½ cup green scallions, chopped
- ½ cup green scallions, sliced lengthwise into 2 inch pieces
- ½ cup uncooked green crab roe & mustard (see page 55)
- 6 peeled plum tomatoes, cored & quartered lengthwise
- fried tofu, 6-8 oz, slices
- 2 tsp salt
- 1 ½ Tbsp fish sauce (nước mắm in Vietnamese)
- ¾ to 1 oz rock sugar (đường phèn in Vietnamese)
- 1 rice stick package, cooked (bún in Vietnamese)

Sides & Garnishes

- water spinach (rau muống in Vietnamese), finely shredded
- banana blossom (bắp chuối in Vietnamese), finely shredded
- bean sprouts (gía in Vietnamese)
- mint (rau húng in Vietnamese)
- Thai basil (rau quế in Vietnamese)
- green or purple perilla (shiso in Japanese or rau tía tô in Vietnamese)
- culantro (rau ngò gai in Vietnamese)
- Vietnamese mint or balm (rau kinh giới in Vietnamese)
- Vietnamese coriander (rau răm in Vietnamese)
- lime wedges (to squeeze into the soup)
- hot chili peppers, chopped
- dollop of fine shrimp sauce (mắm ruốc or mắm tôm in Vietnamese)
- additional fish sauce (nước mắm)
- optional: ½ cup fresh green crab meat (see page 43)

Annatto Oil

INSTRUCTIONS

Prepare Annatto Oil

1. In a pan, add annatto seeds and oil. Stir the seeds over 1-2 minutes, or until the oil turns bright orange-red.

2. Remove the pan from heat and let the seeds steep for about 10-15 minutes.

3. Strain and discard the seeds.

Prepare Crabs

4. Wash the live crabs in cold water and drain.

5. Remove and discard the carapace, gills, and apron. For female crabs, remove the roe and reserve (see page 55 for photos).

   Note: See tips for preparing live crabs on page 16.

6. Clean the crabs again by sprinkling about 2 tsp of salt on the prepared crabs and gently rubbing them.

7. Wash the crabs in cold water 2-3 times to remove the salt. Let them drain in a strainer.

Prepare Broth & Noodle Soup

8. Double bag the crabs in freezer bags (add a handful of crabs at a time to making crushing easier), remove the air and partially seal them, then crush with a heavy object.

   Note: You may alternatively use a food processor to accomplish the same goal.

9. Place the crushed crabs in a large container. Add 4 cups of the cold water and stir the crabs for about 30-40 seconds. Using a fine strainer, strain and filter out the fine crab meat and crab liquid into a large stock pot.

   Note: The fine crab meat will go through the strainer.

10. Add 4 more cups of water to the crushed crabs and repeat the filtration process until all 12 cups of water are used up. By the 3rd time, the crab liquid will become more clear with less crab bits.

11. Save the strained fine crab bits and crab liquid to cook in the same pot. Set the pot aside while cooking the other ingredients. Discard the shell bits and remaining unfiltered crab.

12. Heat a large pan over medium-high heat and add annatto oil. Once the oil is hot, add shallot, garlic, and chopped scallion. Sauté for about 1-2 minutes or until the shallot is soft.

13. Add the roe/crab mustard and sauté for about a minute.

14. Add the tomatoes and tofu and sauté for another minute to coat everything then remove from heat and set aside.

15. Heat the pot with the fine crab bits and crab liquid over medium-high to high heat. Do not stir and let the meat pieces float to the surface undisturbed.

16. Let the broth come to a gentle boil. Once the meat pieces stop floating to the top (about 4-5 minutes), stir once.

    Note: Over-stirring will break the meat into smaller pieces.

17. Add the sautéed contents and sugar to the stock pot. Turn the heat up to medium-high and bring the stock to a gentle boil.

    Note: The rock sugar may take some time to dissolve.

18. Add the 2-inch cut scallions. Season with salt and fish sauce. Turn the heat to very low until ready to serve.

19. Serve piping hot with rice noodles, green crab meat, a platter of herbs and vegetables, additional fish sauce, and fine shrimp sauce on the side.

To make ahead of time, prepare ingredients separately and store individually in the fridge. When ready to serve, bring the stock to a boil and add additional ingredients. Garnish with fresh vegetables, herbs and sauces.

PORTUGESE STYLE

GREEN CRAB STEW

BY CHEF NED GRIEG OF WOODMAN'S OF ESSEX

Woodman's has been known for clams ever since "Chubby" Woodman whipped up some of the first fried clams in 1916. Decades later, when soft-shell clam populations plummeted with green crab predation, Woodman's began cooking with the crab in collaboration with our project. This award-winning spin on their classic recipe uses green crab broth as a base, giving the stew a powerful savory punch.

INGREDIENTS

- 4 Tbsp Spanish olive oil
- 1 cup Spanish onion, thinly sliced
- 1 cup fennel, thinly sliced
- 4 cloves garlic, sliced

- 4 cups whole, peeled plum tomatoes
- ¾ lb baby portobello mushrooms
- 1 cup white wine
- 1 oz basil

- 1-2 Tbsp Spanish paprika
- 1-2 Tbsp turmeric
- kosher salt to taste
- black pepper to taste

- 25 whole baby clams, steamed & shucked
- ¾ lb shrimp, peeled & deveined
- ¾ lb scallops
- ¾ lb linguiça sausage

- 2 Tbsp olive oil
- 1 quart green crab stock (see page 50)
- optional: crusty Portuguese bread & aioli

INSTRUCTIONS

1. In a heavy bottom stock pot, combine the first 4 ingredients and simmer for 5 minutes.

2. Add the next 4 ingredients and 1 cup of green crab broth. Simmer for 15 minutes, gradually adding turmeric, paprika, and a pinch of salt.

3. Add in the meat and seafood and toss until well coated.

4. Sear the meat and seafood in a pan with 1 Tbsp of olive oil until amber brown.

5. Add the remaining stock and simmer for 8-10 minutes. Season with salt and pepper to taste. Serve with aioli & crusty Portuguese bread.

tastings

GOLDEN CAVIAR PÂTÉ

WITH GINGER & MARROW

BY THANH THÁI

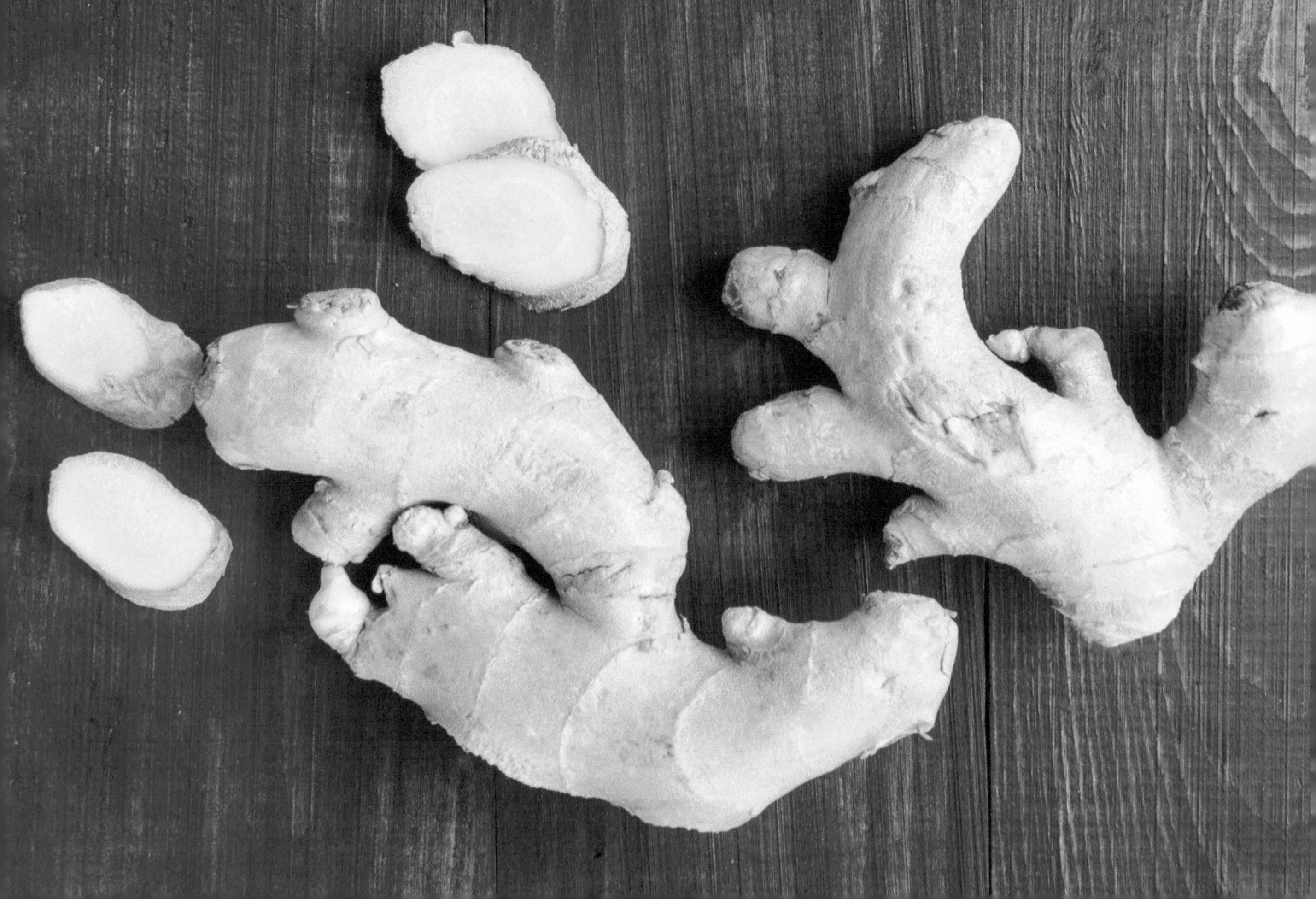

INGREDIENTS

- 2 Tbsp beef marrow
- 1 tsp light olive or vegetable oil
- 1 Tbsp shallot, minced
- 2 Tbsp green scallion, finely chopped
- 1 tsp garlic, grated
- ¼ tsp ginger, grated
- 4 oz cooked roe (masinette in Venetian; see page 26)
- 1 tsp rice wine or sherry
- 2 Tbsp milk or heavy cream
- 1 tsp fish sauce (nước mắm in Vietnamese)
- pinch of sugar
- pinch of freshly ground white pepper

INSTRUCTIONS

1. Place the beef bone marrow in a small pot and add just enough water to submerge the bone. Boil for about 5-7 minutes (depending on the size of the bone) or until the marrow can easily be removed from the bone. Remove the marrow with a chopstick or long narrow spoon once it's cool enough to handle, then set aside.

2. If you are using whole white peppercorns, roast them in a pan over medium high heat for about a minute to enhance the flavor. Grind or crush the peppercorns once cooled and set aside.

3. In a medium-sized pan, heat the marrow and oil over medium-high heat. Then add shallot, green scallion, garlic, and ginger and sauté for about a minute or until the shallot is soft.

4. Add masinette, wine, and, milk. Adjust the heat as needed during cooking. Season with fish sauce, sugar and ground pepper. Cook for about 4-5 minutes to cook off the wine and to reduce some of the liquid.

5. Once the contents cool slightly, pour everything into a food processor and pulse 4-5 times.

6. You can use the pâté immediately or seal and keep in the refrigerator for up to 5 days. Seal well and keep in the freezer up to a month.

OYSTERS & GREEN CRAB

3 WAYS

BY THANH THÁI

OYSTERS ON THE
HALF SHELL

WITH GREEN CRAB MEAT & MASINETTE

INGREDIENTS

- 8 fresh oysters
- cocktail sauce to taste
- sriracha sauce to taste
- masinette & meat shucked from about 8 cooked crabs (see pages 26 & 43)
- sake

INSTRUCTIONS

1. Shuck oysters and avoid spilling the juice. Remove and discard any shell bits.
2. Add about ½ tsp of cocktail sauce and 1-2 drops of sriracha & on each oyster.
3. Add about ½ - 1 tsp of crab meat (and roe if you have any) on top and drizzle about ½ Tbsp of sake over each oyster.

Green Crabs & Oysters: Oyster reefs across the world, from Cape Cod to Southern Australia, are vulnerable to green crab predation.

GRILLED OYSTERS

WITH MASINETTE & SCALLIONS

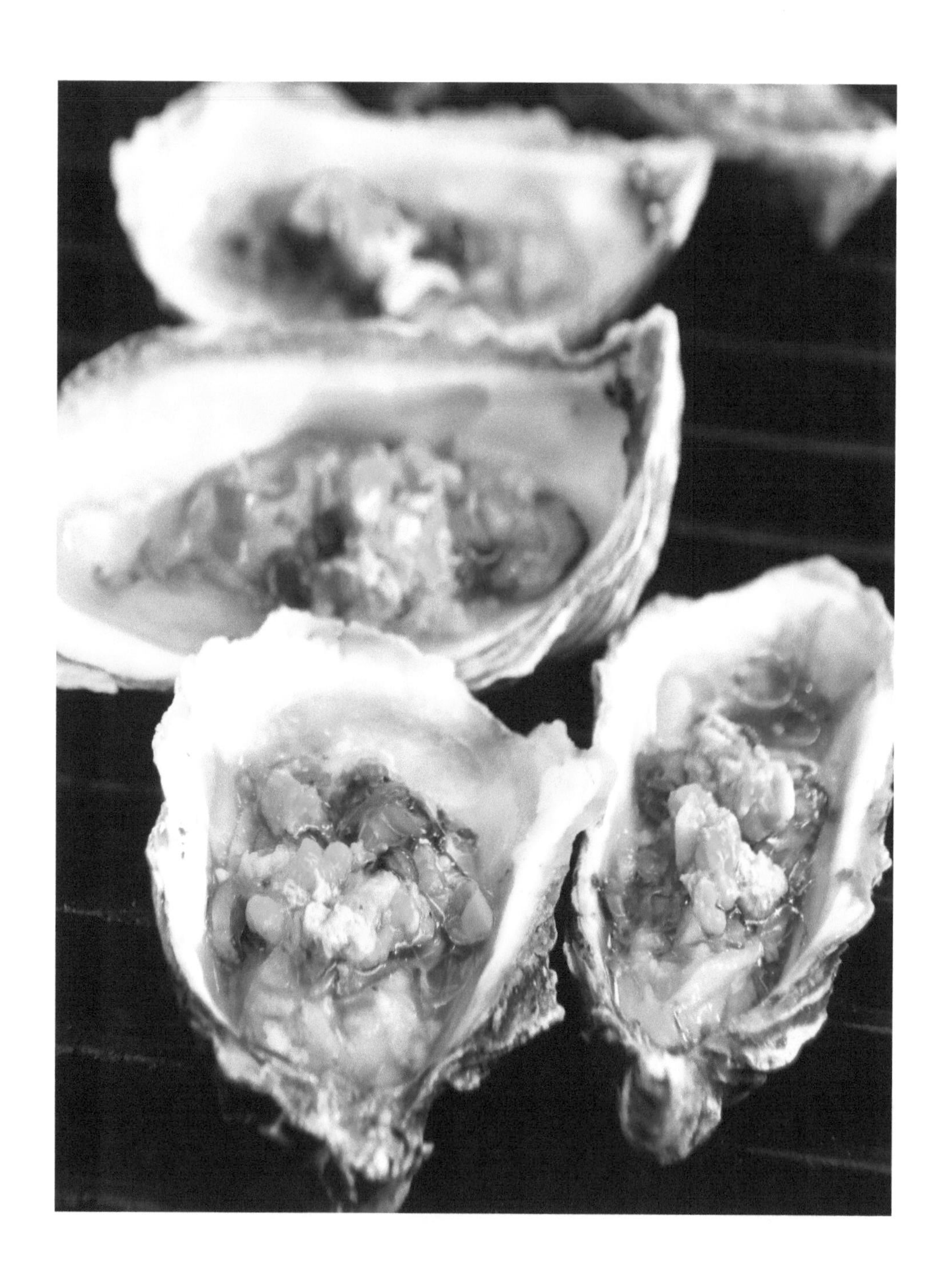

INGREDIENTS

- 8 oysters
- 1 green scallion blade, chopped
- 1 garlic clove, grated
- ½ medium sized shallot, minced
- masinette shucked from 8 cooked crabs (see page 26)
- 1 Tbsp canola or olive oil
- 3 Tbsp white wine
- optional: hot chili pepper, deseeded & chopped

INSTRUCTIONS

1. Preheat grill to medium-high.

2. Shuck the oysters and remove/discard any shell bits. Sprinkle a little of the scallion, garlic, shallot, masinette, and chili pepper on each oyster. Drizzle with a little oil and white wine (about 1 tsp of wine for each oyster).

3. Layer oysters on the grill like shown in the photo . Grill for 2-5 minutes (depending on preference).

OYSTER & CRAB SHOOTER

WITH GREEN CRAB MEAT

INGREDIENTS

- 1 tsp cocktail sauce
- 1 whole raw oyster, freshly shucked
- 1 dash sriracha sauce
- ½ Tbsp cooked green crab meat (see page 43)
- lime juice
- 1 Tbsp of vodka

INSTRUCTIONS

1. Add ½ tsp of cocktail sauce in the glass.

2. Layer with an oyster and its juice, the rest of the cocktail sauce, sriracha sauce, and crab meat.

3. Add a drizzle of lime juice and then vodka. Cheers!

TARAMOSALATA

BY HEATHER ATWOOD OF FOOD FOR THOUGHT

"Taramosalata" is a Greek meze traditionally made with salted carp, mullet, or cod roe. This creamy, flavorful dip is traditionally eaten with other meze and an assortment of vegetables and pita. Taramosalata is typically served in a wide, shallow bowl and drizzled with olive oil.

INGREDIENTS

- 8 ounces crusty white bread, roughly chopped
- ½ cup masinette, sautéed (see page 26)
- 1 small onion, grated
- ⅓ cup lemon juice
- ½ cup olive oil, plus more for drizzling on top
- salt, pepper, & pinch of red pepper flakes

INSTRUCTIONS

1. Put the bread in a medium bowl and pour cold water over the top. Drain immediately and squeeze the excess water out of the bread.

2. Put the bread in the bowl of a food processor fitted with a steel blade. Add the masinette and onion and process lightly. Slowly pour in the lemon juice and olive oil, allowing the bread to slowly soak up the olive oil. Taste for lemon juice, salt, and pepper. Add red pepper flakes and taste again.

3. Transfer to a bowl and smooth out the top of the spread. Drizzle with some additional olive oil and serve with crackers, celery, radish, and carrots. This can be made 2-3 hours in advance. Store in refrigerator and take out 15 minutes before.

ZUCCHINI FLOWERS
STUFFED & FRIED

BY THANH THÁI

I love the idea of stuffing flowers with a filling—either meat, seafood, vegetables, or a combination. Once harvested, the flowers should be used immediately since they tend to wilt or bruise quickly. These fried stuffed zucchini flowers are filled with scallops, shrimp, and the roe of 10 green crabs. You can eat them as they are or with your favorite sauce. I prefer eating them on a bed of fresh home-grown garden herbs and vegetables with a drizzle of the Seasoned Black Bean Sauce or Nước Tương (recipe on page 108).

INGREDIENTS

- 3 oz fresh sea scallops
- 3 oz fresh shrimp
- uncooked roe from 10 green crabs, strained (see page 55)
- 2 Tbsp chopped Chinese chives or scallions
- 2 tsp tapioca or corn starch
- ½ tsp fish sauce (nước mắm in Vietnamese)
- ½ tsp porcini mushroom powder (optional)
- large pinch of ground white or black pepper
- 10 fresh zucchini flowers
- 1 large egg, whisked
- ½ cup masa harina (corn flour)
- a pinch of salt
- oil for deep frying
- optional: seasoned black bean sauce (nước tương in Vietnamese; see page 108)

INSTRUCTIONS

1. Rinse and trim zucchini flowers, leaving ½ inch stem to make dipping easier. Remove and discard the flower stamen.

2. To create the filling, add scallops, shrimp, roe, chives, tapioca/corn starch, fish sauce, mushroom powder, and pepper to a food processor. Pulse a few times to blend all the ingredients. Cover and refrigerate if not using immediately.

3. Whisk an egg in a bowl and set aside. Sift or mix the corn flour and salt onto a plate. Stuff each flower with the filling and set aside.

4. Heat about 3-inches of oil in a pot or a deep fryer. Once the oil heats up to about 350°- 375°, dip one of the stuffed flowers into the whisked egg, shake gently to remove any excess egg . Dip only one at a time to prevent clumping up with too much flour. Dredge the flower in seasoned flour and gently shake off any excess.

5. Gently drop flowers into hot oil, turning a few times to cook evenly, and fry for 3-4 minutes or until golden brown. Only fry 1-2 flowers per time to prevent crowding the pot, which can decrease oil temperature. Remove them from the pot or fryer and place them on paper towels to remove excess oil.

6. Serve hot.

mains

FRIED GREEN CRAB
PO' BOY

BY THANH THÁI

One of my favorite foods from New Orleans is the Po' Boy. These sandwiches are often stuffed with shredded lettuce, sliced tomato, sauce, and fried seafood such as shrimp, soft-shell crab or oysters. The key to this recipe is toasting the roll by frying the interior with a little butter in a skillet. This prevents the sandwich from getting soggy and holds in the savory rémoulade and fried crab.

INGREDIENTS

Po' Boy (Serves 2)

- 1 ½ cup finely shredded lettuce
- 1 large tomato, thinly sliced
- 2 sub rolls, sliced ¾ lengthwise
- 6 fried soft-shell green crabs (see page 39)
- rémoulade (see recipe below)

Rémoulade (Makes 1 ¼ cup)

- 1 cup mayonnaise
- ¼ tsp paprika (preferably sweet kind)
- 2 tsp mustard
- 1 garlic clove, grated
- 1 tsp sriracha sauce
- 1 Tbsp capers, minced
- 2 slices sweet bread & butter chips, chopped
- 1 Tbsp sweet bread & butter chip juice
- 1 Tbsp fresh chives, chopped
- 1 Tbsp onion or shallot, minced

For an Added Umami Punch: Try reducing some of our green crab stock (see page 50) until thickened to make a green crab umami sauce. Then add 1-2 tablespoons to the rémolaude, blending gradually.

INSTRUCTIONS

1. Make the rémoulade by mixing all ingredients. Cover and keep refrigerated.

2. Shred the lettuce and slice the tomato, cover and keep refrigerated. Heat a skillet and melt a pat (about ½ to 1 tablespoon) of butter.

3. Slice the rolls lengthwise about ¾ of the way, leaving a hinge so the 2 halves remain attached.

4. Fry the rolls with the interior facing the bottom of a skillet. Once the interior is golden, remove from heat and set aside.

5. Fry the crabs, following directions on page 39.

6. Spread some of the rémoulade (as much as you prefer) on both sides of the interior of each roll.

7. Layer on the tomato slices, fried crabs, and lettuce. Serve while the crabs are still hot and crispy.

You may save extra rémoulade in a sealed container for later use. Store for up to 5 days in the fridge.

CUA RANG MUỐI

VIETNAMESE SALT & PEPPER CRAB

BY THANH THÁI

INGREDIENTS

Salt & Pepper Crab

- 35 (1 to 1 ½-inches) hard-shell green crabs
- ⅓ cup cornstarch
- ¼ tsp salt
- ¼ tsp ground black or white pepper
- ⅛ tsp turmeric powder
- ⅛ tsp sugar
- oil for deep frying
- 2 tsp vegetable oil
- ½ medium white or yellow onion, peeled and cut into wedges
- ⅓ cup chopped green scallions
- 1 large garlic clove, finely grated

Salt & Pepper Seasoning

- ¼ tsp salt
- ¼ tsp pepper
- ¼ tsp sugar

Cabbage & Mint Salad

- ½ small red cabbage, finely shredded
- 10-15 large fresh mint leaves, julienned
- juice from ½ fresh lime

INSTRUCTIONS

1. Wash the live crabs in cold water.

2. Remove and discard the carapace, gills, mouth-piece, apron, intestine, and pointy distal end of the legs (see photos on next page). For female crabs, leave the roe intact in the bodies.

   Note: See tips for preparing live crabs on page 16.

3. Clean the crabs by sprinkling about 2 tsp of salt on the prepared crabs and gently rubbing them.

4. Wash in cold water 2-3 times to remove the salt. Let them drain in a strainer.

5. Heat the oil until the temperature reaches 350° to 375°.

6. Use a 1-gallon bag or a large container with a lid to mix cornstarch, salt, pepper, turmeric, and sugar.

7. Shake the bag or whisk the contents in the container to mix all of the ingredients.

8. Add the prepared crabs in the bag or container. Shake to coat the crabs with seasoned flour.

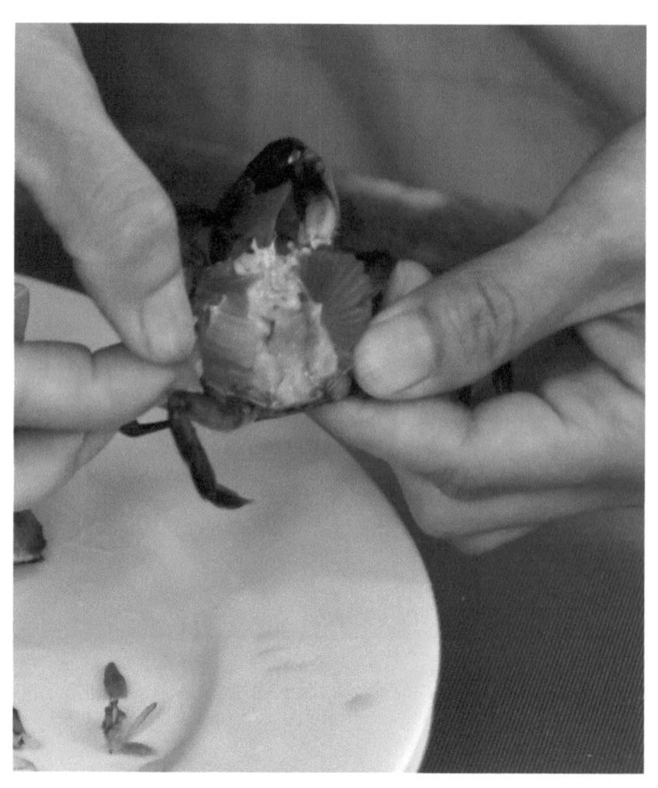

9. Test the oil by dropping in a leg. If the leg sizzles and fries quickly then the oil is hot and ready.

10. Add about 5 crabs at a time to the oil. Fry until they are golden, about 2 ½ to 3 minutes and remove them onto paper towels to remove excess oil.

11. In a large pan or wok, add about 2 teaspoons of oil.

12. Once the oil is hot add onion, scallions, and garlic. Sauté about a minute or until the onion is cooked to your preference.

13. Add the fried crabs to the pan and toss.

14. Slowly add a little of the Salt and Pepper Seasoning and toss the crabs again. Repeat this process until the seasoning has been used up.

15. While crabs are cooling, combine ingredients for the Cabbage and Mint salad.

16. Serve crabs over rice and salad.

BÁNH MÌ CUA

VIETNAMESE CRAB SANDWICHES

BY THANH THÁI

"Bánh mì" is a Vietnamese word that translates to sandwich or sandwiches. In Sóc Trăng, Vietnam sandwiches are made using a few different types of fillings. I grew up eating the classic bánh mì thịt (meat) or bánh mì síu mại (dumplings). The meat could be xá xíu (Chinese barbecued pork) or heo quay (Chinese roast pork from a whole roast pig).

When I was a child living in Vietnam, my mother, who is a jack-of-all-trades, had a portable cart where she sold bánh mì xá xíu. She marinated the meat, grilling it over charcoal for a delicious and fragrant bánh mì filling. She also drizzled a special seasoned bean sauce known in Vietnamese as "nước tương." To this day, I can remember this particular sauce. For years, I returned to Vietnam to visit my late grandmother and often purchased bánh mì thịt, made with the roast pork from a young woman named Nhạn. Her husband roasted whole pigs and she sold the sandwiches in the afternoon after working in the market selling a variety of pork products in the morning. She also used the same bean sauce that I remember from my mother's bánh mì. For my crab sandwiches, I drizzle this sauce over them to recreate the Sóc Trăng style bánh mì that reminds me of my childhood and mother's comfort food.

INGREDIENTS

Seasoned Black Bean Sauce (Nước Tương)

- 2 tsp vegetable oil
- 1 large garlic clove, minced
- 2 Tbsp ground black bean sauce
- 4 Tbsp water
- 2 Tbsp sugar
- 1 scallion blade, chopped

Vietnamese Pickled Vegetables (Đồ Chua)

- 2 medium-sized carrots, cut into 2-inch "matchsticks"
- 1 tsp salt
- ⅔ cup water
- ⅓ cup white vinegar
- 2 ½ Tbsp white sugar

Sandwich (Bánh Mì)

- 1 freshly crisped baguette
- 30 fried soft-shell green crabs (see page 39)
- ½ English cucumber, thinly sliced ⅛ inch thick lengthwise
- 1 small bunch of fresh cilantro
- 1 thinly sliced red onion (soaked in cold water & blotted with paper towel)
- sriracha sauce or hot chili pepper slices
- optional: ½ cup golden caviar pâté (see page 80)

INSTRUCTIONS

Prepare Nước Tương

1. Sauté the garlic in oil until slightly golden.

2. Add ground black bean sauce, water, sugar and scallions.

3. Cook on medium-low heat for about 5 minutes.

Prepare Đồ Chua

4. Prepare Carrots: Peel and cut the carrots into 2-inch matchsticks, sprinkle with salt and let them sit for about 15 minutes to help remove some excess water. Wash in cold water and let everything drain.

5. Prepare Brine: Cook the water, vinegar, and sugar in a small pot until the sugar dissolved. Gently simmer the liquid for about 2-3 minutes. Let it cool down completely.

6. Pickle: Place the prepared carrots in a glass jar or ceramic bowl. Pour the cooled brine over it. Seal the jar or bowl.

Prepare Baguette

7. Spray the top of the baguette with a little water and place it in a preheated oven at 375° for about 7-8 minutes or until it is slightly firm to touch.

Assemble Bánh Mì

8. For a traditional sandwich, cut the baguette into 3 or 6-inch pieces lengthwise about ¾ of the way, leaving a hinge so the 2 halves remain attached. Spread a few spoonfuls of Golden Caviar Pâté on each side, place 1-2 strips cucumber on one side, place 2-3 fried soft-shell green crabs in the middle, stuff with đồ chua, onion and cilantro, and drizzle with nước tương and sriracha sauce.

9. For an open-faced appetizer, slice the baguette into ½-inch thick round slices. Spread about ½ to 1 tablespoon of golden caviar pâté on each slice. Top with đồ chua, sliced onion, a fried green crab, fresh cilantro and drizzle with nước tương and sriracha sauce.

I recommend you prepare all of your ingredients ahead of time except for frying the crabs and crisping the baguette. Wash all the herbs and vegetables and put them in the refrigerator so they will stay fresh. Once you have the last 2 ingredients, then you can quickly assemble the Bánh Mì.

MASINETTE CRAB CAKES

WITH SWEET POTATO

BY MARY PARKS

"Masinette" or green crab caviar, is known for its intense and complex flavor profile and texture. Combined with sweet potato and caraway seeds, masinette can be used to create an incredible crab cake that satisfies sweet and savory senses. The crab cakes can be served as an appetizer, side, or main course. To enjoy masinette crab cakes after the fall and winter season, freeze the cakes on parchment paper and then transfer to a sealed container to freeze for up to three months. Caviar can also be sealed and frozen for up to three months.

INGREDIENTS

Crab Cakes

- 1 cup baked sweet potato
- ⅓ cup fresh masinette (see page 26)
- splash of white wine
- 1 shallot, minced
- 2 cloves garlic, minced
- 3 sprigs basil
- 3 sprigs parsley
- ¼ tsp caraway seed
- 1 tsp lemon zest
- 2 medium-sized eggs
- ½ cup unseasoned breadcrumbs
- 1 tsp salt
- ~3 Tbsp olive oil

Dill Cream

- 4 oz sour cream
- 2 Tbsp lemon juice
- 3 Tbsp fresh dill, chopped
- 1 pinch sea salt

INSTRUCTIONS

1. Preheat oven to 425° and prick the sweet potatoes with a fork to release steam. Bake 1-3 sweet potatoes for 45 minutes and let cool. Scrape baked potato into a bowl and mash.

2. Simmer the shallot and garlic in oil on low heat until translucent, add masinette and a splash of white wine. Remove from heat when the wine has reduced.

3. Whisk an egg for 1 minute then slowly add masinette, sweet potato, herbs, spices, lemon zest, and breadcrumbs.

4. Combine mixture with hands to evenly blend.

5. The cake's texture should resemble a very soft cookie dough. If needed, continue to slowly add breadcrumbs until you are able to form a loose 1 inch ball with the mixture.

6. Distribute 1 inch balls along a parchment lined baking sheet and gently press to form 2 inch diameter patties.

7. Gently coat cakes in a layer of eggs and another layer of breadcrumbs and chill in the fridge for 20 minutes.

8. Heat skillet with ½ inch of oil on medium high heat.

9. Cook cakes in small batches of no more than 3 cakes, turning every 1-2 minutes until each side is brown.

10. While the cakes cool on a rack, prepare the dill cream by mixing the dill, sour cream, fresh lemon juice and a pinch of sea salt.

Crab cakes with braised mustard greens, poached eggs, dill cream, and pickled vegetables

GREEN CRAB SANDWICH

WITH SIGNATURE BUTTER SAUCE

BY THANH THÁI

When I first immigrated to the United States in 1980, my mother came up with this signature butter sauce. I think the recipe was my mother's way of helping our family become acclimated to the American ways of life, food, and culture. We use this delicious sauce (sometimes with moderation and sometimes not) to dip or drizzle over our lobsters, crabs, steamers and other seafood. I honestly believe that just about everything tastes better with fish sauce!

INGREDIENTS

Sandwich

- 1 hamburger bun, toasted
- 2-3 oz of freshly picked green crab meat & roe (masinette in Venetian; see pages 26 & 43)
- signature butter sauce (see recipe below)
- optional: Thai basil and shiso flowers

Signature Butter Sauce (Makes ¼ cup)

- 3 Tbsp unsalted or salted butter
- ½ tsp fish sauce (nước mắm in Vietnamese)
- ½ tsp sugar
- 2 Tbsp green scallions, chopped

INSTRUCTIONS

1. **Prepare Signature Butter Sauce:** Mix butter, fish sauce, sugar and scallions in a small saucepan. Cook until the butter has melted. Or add all ingredients in a microwavable bowl and microwave for 20-30 minutes or until the butter has melted.

2. **Prepare Sandwich:** Divide the crab meat and roe then add between toasted buns. Drizzle with the butter sauce and garnish with flowers.

MASINETTE & LINGUINE

BY MARY PARKS

In Venice, masinette is often served atop linguine with a drizzle of olive oil and fresh cracked pepper. Rich, savory, and beautifully simple, this dish is a crowd pleaser.

INGREDIENTS

- ½ cup fresh masinette (see page 26)
- juice & zest of 1 lemon or splash of white wine
- 3 Tbsp olive oil (for skillet)
- salt, pepper and marjoram to taste

INSTRUCTIONS

1. Add linguine to salted, boiling water. Cook for approximately 8 minutes then remove and strain.

2. Add olive oil and marjoram to a large skillet on medium heat. Lightly sauté masinette for 2 minutes then add lemon zest.

3. Reduce with lemon juice or white wine then add freshly cracked pepper and salt to taste.

4. Toss pasta for one to 2 minutes in skillet and serve!

CAMPARI & TARRAGON

LINGUINE WITH GREEN CRAB BROTH

BY SOLÓN ARGÜELLO & MARY PARKS

Adding green crab stock to pastas and risottos is a great way of incorporating the crab's umami elements without overpowering other flavors. In developing this recipe, we found the sharp tarragon and acidic campari tomatoes perfectly contrasted the savory and rich flavor of the green crab stock. This recipe can be enjoyed any time of year and comes together in minutes. We recommend using fresh tarragon and experimenting with French, Mexican, and Russian varieties.

INGREDIENTS

- ½ cup green crab broth (see page 50)
- 3 Tbsp olive oil for skillet
- 12 quartered campari tomatoes
- 4 cloves minced garlic
- fresh tarragon to taste (chopped)
- splash of white wine
- salt, pepper, and dried thyme to taste

INSTRUCTIONS

1. With a large skillet on medium heat, add tomatoes and a splash of olive oil and simmer for 6 – 8 minutes.
2. When tomatoes begin to loose shape, create a "mote" with the sauce. In the center, add garlic and additional olive oil.
3. Reduce with a splash of white wine and thyme. After reduced, season with salt and pepper.
4. Add green crab broth and reduce until sauce reaches desired consistency.
5. To salted, boiling water add linguine & cook for approximately 8 minutes. Strain pasta, reserving 1 tablespoon of starchy pasta water.
6. Add cooked pasta to skillet and 1 tablespoon of pasta water, toss in chopped tarragon.
7. Toss pasta for 1 or 2 minutes in the skillet and serve!

GRILLED PIZZA
WITH SMALL FRIED GREEN CRABS

BY THANH THÁI

INGREDIENTS

- 1 pizza dough
- 30 tiny live crabs (less than 1 inch)
- 1 large sized tomato, thinly sliced
- sliced pepper jack, mozzarella, or cheese of choice
- 1 red onion, thinly sliced
- vegetables of choice

INSTRUCTIONS

1. Fry the crabs in oil for about 10 seconds. Scoop them onto paper towels to remove excess oil.

   Note: With a thinner shell, smaller hardshell crabs are great for deep frying. The result is a crunchy bite-sized morsel.

2. Preheat the oven to the highest possible temperature (around 500°-550° if possible) with a pizza stone (if you have one).

3. Dust the surface of your working area (use a pizza peel if possible) with plenty of flour before placing the dough down. Roll the dough out to a desired thickness.

4. Dab tomato slices on a clean paper towel to remove excess liquid before scattering them on the pizza. This will help prevent the pizza from getting too soggy.

5. Layer the cheese and arrange the crabs. Then layer veggies and slices of red onion.

6. Bake for about 10 minutes or until the pizza crust is golden. In the final minute, add a few more slices of cheese and turn off heat.

about the **authors**

Mary Parks

Mary has a background in sustainable fisheries, developing underutilized and invasive species and leading environmental compliance programs for commercial seafood companies. She hails from coastal Maine and first tried eating green crabs in 2005. Over a decade later, she helped found the Green Crab R&D Project, a nonprofit dedicated to green crab culinary development. Based in Boston, she now serves as the organization's Executive Director.

Thanh Thái

Thanh is a family nurse practitioner living in coastal New Hampshire. When she's not seeing patients, she can be found harvesting green crabs and developing recipes. Thanh runs the blog Green Crab Cafe, which explores the vast culinary potential of the invasive crab through diverse recipes and tutorials.

additional resources

The Green Crab R&D Project
greencrab.org
Our nonprofit: new recipes, free resources, and public events

Manomet Green Crabs
manomet.org/project/green-crabs
Project partner: soft-shell green crab development, outreach, and monitoring

NH Seagrant - Green Crab Project
seagrant.unh.edu/nh-green-crab-project
Project partner: citizen science monitoring, soft-shell green crab development, and outreach

Green Crab Cafe
greencrabcafe.com
Project partner: a vast database of recipes and resources by Thanh Thái

Green Crab Nation
greencrabnation.com
Project partner: volume supplier of green crabs

University of Prince Edward Island
projects.upei.ca/cerc/1166-2/
Soft-shell green crab development & monitoring

Washington Seagrant - Green Crab ID
wsg.washington.edu/crabteam/greencrab/id/
Identification information & green crabs on the West Coast

Cohen et al., 1995
Published in Marine Biology
Introduction, dispersal and potential impacts of the green crab *Carcinus maenas* in San Francisco Bay, California

CPSIA information can be obtained
at www.ICGtesting.com
Printed in the USA
BVHW091336180819
555577BV00006B/3/P

9780578427942